W9-BWU-581

Date: 2/13/12

J 575.4 BOD
Bodach, Vijaya.
Stems /

Pebble® Plus

Plant Parts

Stems

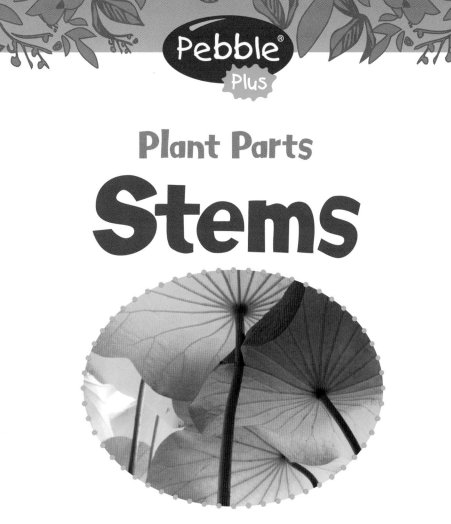

by Vijaya Khisty Bodach

Consulting Editor: Gail Saunders-Smith, PhD

Consultant: Judson R. Scott, Current President
American Society of Consulting Arborists

Capstone press®

Mankato, Minnesota

Pebble Plus is published by Capstone Press,
151 Good Counsel Drive, P.O. Box 669, Mankato, Minnesota 56002.
www.capstonepub.com

Books published by Capstone Press are manufactured with paper
containing at least 10 percent post-consumer waste.

Library of Congress Cataloging-in-Publication Data
Bodach, Vijaya Khisty.
    Stems / by Vijaya Khisty Bodach.
       p. cm.—(Pebble plus. Plant parts)
    Summary: "Simple text and photographs present the stems of plants, how they grow, and their
uses"—Provided by publisher.
    Includes bibliographical references and index.
    ISBN-13: 978-0-7368-6347-6 (hardcover)
    ISBN-10: 0-7368-6347-8 (hardcover)
    ISBN-13: 978-0-7368-9624-5 (softcover pbk.)
    ISBN-10: 0-7368-9624-4 (softcover pbk.)
    1. Stems (Botany)—Juvenile literature. I. Title. II. Series.
QK646.B63 2007
575.4—dc22   2006000995

Editorial Credits
Sarah L. Schuette, editor; Jennifer Bergstrom, designer; Kelly Garvin, photo researcher/photo editor

Photo Credits
Capstone Press/Karon Dubke, cover, 5
Dwight R. Kuhn, 6–7, 12–13, 15 (inset), 22 (all)
Peter Arnold/David Cavagnaro, 18–19
Shutterstock/Alexey Lisovoy, 10–11; Lancelot et Naelle, 14–15; Rudolf Georg, 20–21; Sirano 100, 1; zastavkin, 9
Visuals Unlimited/Inga Spence, 16–17

Note to Parents and Teachers

The Plant Parts set supports national science standards related to identifying plant
parts and the diversity and interdependence of life. This book describes and illustrates
stems. The images support early readers in understanding the text. The repetition of
words and phrases helps early readers learn new words. This book also introduces early
readers to subject-specific vocabulary words, which are defined in the Glossary section.
Early readers may need assistance to read some words and to use the Table of Contents,
Glossary, Read More, Internet Sites, and Index sections of the book.

Printed in the United States of America in North Mankato, Minnesota.
062011   006208R

Table of Contents

Plants Need Stems

Stems join the leaves
and roots of a plant.
Most stems grow
above the soil.

Leaves grow from stems.

Stems hold leaves up

to the sun.

Leaves make food

out of sunlight.

Stems act like straws.

They carry food

from the leaves and roots

to the whole plant.

All Kinds of Stems

Tall, woody tree trunks
are stems covered with bark.
The bark protects the stem.

Strawberry plants have long, thin stems. The stems creep along on top of the soil.

13

Tulip bulbs
are underground stems.
In spring, leaves grow up
and tulips bloom.

bulb

Stems We Eat

Some stems are good to eat.

Celery stems are
a crunchy snack.

Asparagus stems grow quickly.

These stems are called spears.

Wonderful Stems

Woody or soft, thick or thin,
stems help plants stay alive.

Parts of an Oak Tree

Glossary

bulb—an underground stem; tulips grow from bulbs.

leaves—the flat, green parts of a plant that grow out from a stem

root—the part of a plant that grows mostly underground; food gathered by roots moves through stems to the rest of the plant.

soil—the dirt where plants grow; most plants get their food and water from the soil.

Read More

Farndon, John. *Stems.* World of Plants. San Diego: Blackbirch Press, 2005.

Hunter, Rebecca. *The Facts About Flowering Plants.* North Mankato, Minn.: Smart Apple Media, 2005.

Morgan, Sally. *Green Plants.* Life Science In Depth. Chicago: Heinemann Library, 2006.

Index

Word Count: 122
Grade: 1
Early-Intervention Level: 15

Internet Sites

FactHound offers a safe, fun way to find Internet sites related to this book. All of the sites on FactHound have been researched by our staff.

Here's how:

1. Visit *www.facthound.com*

2. Choose your grade level.

3. Type in this book ID **0736863478** for age-appropriate sites. You may also browse subjects by clicking on letters, or by clicking on pictures and words.

4. Click on the **Fetch It** button.

Facthound will fetch the best sites for you!